DAISY P. OLIVER

Tennessee: Travel Guide

Emphasis on Nashville, Gatlinburg and Pigeon Forge (Must See. Must Do. Must Eat!)

Copyright © 2023 by Daisy P. Oliver

All rights reserved. No part of this publication may be reproduced, stored or transmitted in any form or by any means, electronic, mechanical, photocopying, recording, scanning, or otherwise without written permission from the publisher. It is illegal to copy this book, post it to a website, or distribute it by any other means without permission.

Daisy P. Oliver asserts the moral right to be identified as the author of this work.

Daisy P. Oliver has no responsibility for the persistence or accuracy of URLs for external or third-party Internet Websites referred to in this publication and does not guarantee that any content on such Websites is, or will remain, accurate or appropriate.

Designations used by companies to distinguish their products are often claimed as trademarks. All brand names and product names used in this book and on its cover are trade names, service marks, trademarks and registered trademarks of their respective owners. The publishers and the book are not associated with any product or vendor mentioned in this book. None of the companies referenced within the book have endorsed the book.

First edition

This book was professionally typeset on Reedsy.
Find out more at reedsy.com

Contents

1	Introduction	1
2	Planning your trip and what to expect	3
3	Getting settled into accommodations	14
4	Local Barbecue	18
5	Local Restaurants	23
6	Tours	29
7	Local Attractions	36
8	Local Bars	49
9	Nightlife and Live Music	55
10	Family Friendly Activities	60
11	Conclusion	66

1

Introduction

Welcome to the Middle Tennessee Guide Book where we emphasize Nashville, Gatlinburg and Pigeon Forge. Take a journey through the heart of the Volunteer State that promises to be as rich and vibrant as the region itself. In these pages, we'll take you on an exploration of the music, history, food, and culture that make Middle Tennessee a must-visit destination for travelers of all kinds.

Middle Tennessee isn't just a place; it's an experience waiting to be lived. Whether you're a first-time visitor, a frequent traveler, or a local looking for fresh adventures, this guide is your key to unlocking the secrets and delights of this extraordinary region.

As you flip through these pages, prepare to be immersed in the soulful sounds of Nashville's live music scene, tantalized by the mouth watering aromas of the best BBQ joints, and captivated by the diverse history and attractions that await. Whether you're traveling solo, with a partner, family, or a group of friends, Middle Tennessee has something to offer everyone.

With chapters dedicated to practical trip planning, accommodations, the finest local eateries, tours, attractions, nightlife, and family activities, we'll leave no stone unturned. Our aim is to transport you to Middle Tennessee, providing you with insights that will make your visit unforgettable and ensure you discover the region's hidden gems.

So, fasten your seatbelts, sharpen your taste buds, and let the rhythm of Tennessee's music and the aroma of its cuisine guide you through the chapters ahead. It's time to embark on a journey that will leave you yearning for more and eager to explore this dynamic and vibrant slice of the South. Welcome to Middle Tennessee; let's get started.

2

Planning your trip and what to expect

Budgeting for your Trip

Setting a budget for your Middle Tennessee adventure is a pivotal first step in ensuring a memorable and stress-free experience. Here's a breakdown of actionable advice on how to effectively budget for your trip:

Start with a Total Budget: Begin by determining the total amount you're willing to spend on your trip. This should include your flights, accommodation, food, activities, and a contingency fund for unexpected expenses.

Breakdown Your Expenses: Divide your budget into categories, such as transportation, accommodation, food, entertainment, and miscellaneous expenses. This helps you allocate your funds more efficiently.

Research and Estimate Costs: Research the average costs associated with your trip. Look up flight prices, hotel rates, and meal expenses. Consider any entrance fees for attractions you plan to visit. Websites, travel forums, and guidebooks are excellent resources for estimating expenses.

Be Realistic: Ensure your budget is realistic based on your travel style. If you're a budget traveler, keep expenses to a minimum. However, if you prefer more luxurious experiences, be prepared to allocate more funds accordingly.

Include a Contingency Fund: Unforeseen expenses can occur, so it's wise to set aside some extra money for emergencies or unexpected opportunities that might arise during your trip.

Use Travel Apps and Tools: There are numerous apps and websites that can help you monitor your budget while traveling. Tools like budget tracking apps and currency converters can be invaluable in staying on top of your spending.

Cut Costs with Advance Booking: Plan and book your flights, accommodations, and activities in advance. This often allows you to secure better deals and promotions, saving you money in the long run.

Consider All-Inclusive Packages: Some destinations in Middle Tennessee offer all-inclusive packages that cover accommodations, meals, and activities. These can be cost-effective and convenient options for some travelers.

Seek Local Recommendations: Locals often know the best places to eat, stay, and explore that won't break the bank. Engage with residents, explore local forums, or check out blogs and reviews for insider tips on budget-friendly options.

Meal Planning: Dining expenses can add up quickly. Save money by exploring local markets, food trucks, and affordable eateries. Limit dining in upscale restaurants to special occasions.

Public Transportation: If available, use public transportation as it's usually more cost-effective than renting a car or relying on taxis.

Use Travel Rewards and Discounts: Take advantage of frequent flyer miles, hotel loyalty programs, and student or senior discounts when applicable. These can significantly reduce your overall costs.

By following these budgeting tips, you'll have a clearer financial picture of your Middle Tennessee trip and be better equipped to make the most of your experience without overspending. Remember, a well-planned budget ensures you can enjoy all that Middle Tennessee has to offer while keeping your finances in check.

Consider Holidays

Planning your trip to Middle Tennessee around specific holidays can offer a unique and festive experience. Here's a breakdown of actionable advice on how to consider holidays in your travel plans, including what costs to expect and how to make the most of your visit:

Identify Local Holidays and Festivals: Research and identify local holidays, festivals, and events in Middle Tennessee. Check the official tourism websites or local event calendars to see if any coincide with your travel dates.

Plan Ahead: Once you've chosen a holiday or festival to attend, make your travel plans well in advance. Flights, accommodations, and event tickets may get booked up quickly, and prices can rise as the date approaches.

Accommodation Costs: Be prepared for potentially higher accommodation costs during popular holidays or festivals. Consider staying a bit outside the main event area to save on lodging expenses while still being within reach.

Event Tickets: If the holiday or festival you're interested in requires tickets, purchase them early to secure your spot and possibly benefit from early bird discounts.

Local Discounts: Check for special holiday discounts and promotions offered by local businesses, restaurants, and attractions. Many places may have holiday-themed deals.

Transportation: If you're attending a holiday event in a city, consider using public transportation or ride-sharing services to avoid parking costs and traffic congestion.

Cultural Respect: Familiarize yourself with local customs and traditions surrounding the holiday or festival. Being culturally respectful will enhance your experience and ensure you don't inadvertently offend anyone.

Local Advice: Connect with locals or fellow travelers who have experienced the holiday or festival before. They can provide valuable insights and money-saving tips for making the most of your visit.

Booking your Flight

When booking your flight to Middle Tennessee, consider these five essential tips for a cost-effective and convenient journey. First, start your search early to snag the best deals, as airlines often release their most competitive fares months in advance. Second, stay flexible with your travel dates, as flights on certain days or during off-peak seasons tend to be more affordable. Third, use flight search engines like Google Flights and Skyscanner to compare prices and find the most competitive options. Fourth, be open to layovers, as they often lead to lower airfares, and consider nearby airports that might offer more budget-friendly options. Fifth, be aware of baggage fees when comparing fares. Some airlines include baggage in their ticket prices, while others charge extra. Packing light or choosing an airline with favorable baggage policies can save you money. Lastly, sign up for fare alerts to stay in the loop about price drops for your desired route, and don't forget to book on Tuesdays or Wednesdays, historically known for having lower fares.

Bundling your flight, hotel and car rental

When bundling your flight, hotel, and car rental for your Middle Tennessee journey, here are the five best tips to make the most of this approach. First, begin your search on travel booking websites like Expedia, Orbitz, Priceline and Travelocity, where bundled packages are often available. Second, compare the individual costs of flights, hotels, and car rentals to ensure bundling offers genuine savings. Third, check for exclusive discounts and promotions tailored to bundled packages, as these can significantly reduce your overall expenses. Fourth, remain flexible with your travel dates to access a wider range of bundling options, potentially providing you with better value. Lastly, read the fine print carefully, considering cancellation policies, change fees, and any potential restrictions to make an informed decision about your bundled package.

Transportation

Selecting the right transportation method, such as car rental, can greatly impact your exploration.

Book in Advance: Just like with flights and accommodations, booking your car rental in advance can secure better rates and ensure vehicle availability, especially during peak travel seasons.

Use Comparison Websites: Websites like Rentalcars.com, Kayak, and AutoSlash allow you to compare car rental prices from various providers in Middle Tennessee. Utilize these platforms to find the best deals.

Choose the Right Vehicle: Opt for a car size that suits your needs. Smaller, more fuel-efficient cars are often cheaper, but if you're traveling with a group or need space for luggage, consider a larger vehicle.

Insurance Considerations: Check if your personal auto insurance or credit card covers rental car insurance. If it does, you can decline costly rental agency insurance options, saving you money.

Fill up the Tank: Refuel the car yourself before returning it to avoid steep refueling charges from the rental agency. Gas stations near the airport may have higher prices, so plan accordingly.

Check Mileage Limits: Be aware of any mileage restrictions in your rental agreement. If you plan to drive extensively, consider options with unlimited mileage to avoid extra fees.

Membership Discounts: If you're a member of an auto club or loyalty program, check if they offer discounts or benefits when renting a car.

This can lead to significant savings.

One-Way Rentals: If you plan to return the car to a different location, check for one-way rental fees. Sometimes it's more cost-effective to return to your original rental location.

Arriving from outside the US

When arriving in Middle Tennessee from outside the United States, focusing on these five key tips can ensure a smooth transition and a seamless beginning to your journey. Firstly, verify that your passport is valid for at least six months beyond your intended departure date and research the visa requirements for your nationality, ensuring that you apply for a visa well in advance if necessary. Secondly, if you're part of the Visa Waiver Program (VWP), it's essential to apply for the Electronic System for Travel Authorization (ESTA) before your trip, as it is mandatory for pre-screening VWP travelers. Thirdly, familiarize yourself with US customs regulations, especially regarding the declaration of items you're bringing into the country, including duty-free purchases, to avoid potential fines. Upon your arrival at the airport, have your passport, visa (if required), and ESTA authorization ready, and anticipate customs officers' questions and potential lines.

Weather

Middle Tennessee experiences a diverse range of weather conditions throughout the year, making it essential to consider the climate when planning your trip.

Spring (March to May): Spring in Middle Tennessee is a delightful time to visit. The weather gradually warms up, with temperatures typically ranging from the mid-50s°F (12°C) to the mid-70s°F (24°C). You can expect blooming flowers, lush landscapes, and comfortably mild weather. Spring is perfect for outdoor activities, including hiking, exploring parks, and enjoying local events.

Summer (June to August): Summers in Middle Tennessee can be hot and humid. Temperatures often climb into the high 80s°F (30°C) and sometimes surpass 90°F (32°C). Be prepared for occasional thunderstorms and high humidity. It's an excellent season for live music, festivals, and water-related activities, such as boating on the region's lakes and rivers.

Fall (September to November): Autumn is a particularly beautiful time to visit Middle Tennessee. The weather is pleasant, with temperatures ranging from the mid-60s°F (18°C) to the mid-70s°F (24°C). The fall foliage is spectacular, especially in the Great Smoky Mountains. It's an ideal season for hiking, exploring state parks, and enjoying scenic drives.

Winter (December to February): Winters in Middle Tennessee are relatively mild, with temperatures ranging from the high 30s°F (3°C) to the mid-40s°F (7°C). While snow is infrequent, it can occur, particularly in the northern part of the state. Winter is a quieter season, making it suitable for indoor attractions, cozy evenings by the fireplace, and taking advantage of holiday events and festivities.

The best time to visit Middle Tennessee depends on your preferences and the activities you plan to enjoy. Spring and fall are typically the most popular seasons due to the pleasant weather and outdoor recreational opportunities. Summer is perfect for those seeking lively events and water activities, while winter is a peaceful time for those who prefer a quieter, cozy atmosphere. Be sure to check the local weather forecast as you plan your trip to ensure you pack appropriately and make the most of the seasonal offerings in this vibrant region.

How Long to Stay

Determining the ideal duration for your Middle Tennessee visit depends on your interests and the experiences you wish to enjoy.

Weekend Getaway (2-3 Days): If you're looking for a quick escape or have limited time, a weekend getaway can be fulfilling. Spend 2-3 days exploring the highlights, enjoying local cuisine, and taking in some live music in cities like Nashville.

Short Trip (4-5 Days): A 4-5 day trip allows you to delve deeper into the region. You can explore key attractions, embark on a scenic drive, savor more of the local food, and attend live performances or festivals.

A Week or More: To experience Middle Tennessee thoroughly, consider staying for a week or more. This duration allows you to explore multiple cities and attractions, go on outdoor adventures, visit museums, and immerse yourself in local culture and music.

Extended Stay (2 Weeks or More): If you have a passion for music, history, and outdoor activities, consider an extended stay of two weeks or more. This duration enables you to explore Middle Tennessee's diversity in-depth and possibly take side trips to surrounding states.

Remember to tailor your visit to your interests. Whether you're a music enthusiast, history buff, or nature lover, the duration of your stay should align with the experiences you wish to have. Middle Tennessee offers something for every traveler, and the length of your stay can be customized to match your unique preferences.

What to Pack

Packing for your Tennessee adventure should be tailored to the season of your visit. Regardless of the season, be sure to pack essential travel items such as toiletries, chargers, and travel documents, including your passport, visa, and any required permits. Tailoring your packing list to the season will ensure that you're comfortable and well-prepared for the weather and activities during your Middle Tennessee journey.

Spring (March to May): Spring can be unpredictable, so it's wise to pack layers. Bring lightweight clothing, including long-sleeved shirts and sweaters, along with a mix of short-sleeved shirts. Don't forget comfortable walking shoes for outdoor activities. A light jacket and an umbrella can come in handy for occasional rain showers. If you plan to hike, bring appropriate gear and a water-resistant jacket.

Summer (June to August): Summers in Middle Tennessee can be hot and humid, so pack lightweight, breathable clothing, such as shorts, T-shirts, and sundresses. Don't forget a wide-brimmed hat, sunscreen, and sunglasses to protect yourself from the sun. Comfortable, closed-toe shoes are essential for exploring the region. If you plan to visit outdoor attractions, consider bringing a refillable water bottle and insect repellent.

Fall (September to November): Fall is known for its pleasant weather and beautiful foliage. Pack a variety of clothing for layering, including long-sleeved shirts, sweaters, and light jackets. Comfortable walking shoes are crucial for outdoor adventures and exploring state parks.

Don't forget a camera to capture the stunning fall colors.

Winter (December to February): Winters in Middle Tennessee are relatively mild, but it's advisable to pack warmer clothing. Bring a mix of sweaters, long-sleeved shirts, and a heavy coat. Comfortable walking shoes with good traction are essential if you plan to explore outdoor attractions. A pair of gloves, a hat, and a scarf can help keep you warm during cooler evenings.

3

Getting settled into accommodations

Transportation from the Airport to Hotel

Upon landing, you'll need to find your way to your accommodation. If you've booked a rental car, great! If not, here are considerations:

Airport Shuttle Services: Many airports in Middle Tennessee offer shuttle services that can transport you directly to popular hotels and destinations. These shuttles are typically cost-effective, with prices ranging from $15 to $30 per person, depending on the specific route and distance to your hotel. They are convenient and often operate on a regular schedule.

Taxi and Ride-Sharing Services: Taxis and ride-sharing services like Uber and Lyft are readily available at Middle Tennessee airports. Prices may vary depending on the distance to your hotel, traffic conditions, and time of day. On average, expect to pay between $20 and $50 for a one-way trip to your hotel. These services provide flexibility in choosing your destination and can accommodate multiple passengers.

Hotel Shuttle Services: Many hotels in the area provide complimentary shuttle services to and from the airport. These services are often free of charge for hotel guests, adding convenience to your stay. Make sure to check with your hotel in advance to confirm availability and schedule your pick-up.

Limousines and Private Car Services: If you're looking for a more luxurious and comfortable experience, consider booking a private limousine or car service. Prices vary depending on the vehicle type and service provider, but you can expect to pay between $50 and $200 for a one-way trip to your hotel. These services offer personalized transportation and are ideal for special occasions or when you want a hassle-free experience.

When deciding on the best transportation option, consider factors such as your budget, the location of your hotel, the number of passengers, and your personal preferences. Each choice offers a different experience, and selecting the one that aligns with your needs will ensure a smooth and enjoyable start to your Middle Tennessee journey.

Managing Time Difference and Jet Lag

Middle Tennessee, follows the Central Time Zone (CT) during Standard Time.

Adjust Your Clock: As soon as you arrive in Nashville, set your watch, phone, and other timekeeping devices to the local time. This immediate adjustment can help your body align with the new time zone.

Stick to Local Schedules: Begin eating and sleeping according to Nashville's local time as soon as you arrive. This will help your body adapt to the region's rhythms and reduce the disorientation caused by the time difference.

Stay Active and Get Sunlight: Engaging in light physical activity, like taking a walk, and spending time outdoors during daylight hours is beneficial. Exposure to natural light helps reset your circadian rhythms, making it easier for your body to adjust to the local time.

Stay Hydrated and Limit Caffeine and Alcohol: Adequate hydration is essential for adapting to a new time zone. Restrict your intake of caffeine and alcohol, as these substances can disrupt your sleep patterns and exacerbate the effects of jet lag.

Consider Short Naps: While it's generally recommended to avoid napping upon arrival, if you're extremely fatigued, a short power nap of around 20-30 minutes can provide a quick energy boost without interfering with your ability to sleep at night.

Provisioning: supermarket food options

When it comes to provisioning and finding non-restaurant food options in Middle Tennessee, you'll have a variety of local and chain supermarkets to choose from to stock up on essentials like bottled water, fresh fruits, snacks, and easy-to-prepare meals to make your stay comfortable and cost-effective. Here's a list of some popular options in the region:

Local & Chain Supermarkets:

- Piggly Wiggly
- Kroger

GETTING SETTLED INTO ACCOMMODATIONS

- Publix
- Walmart
- Target
- ALDI
- Costco
- Safeway

4

Local Barbecue

This chapter delves into the rich culinary tradition of Tennessee, with a focus on the best barbecue joints in Nashville, Gatlinburg, and Pigeon Forge. It provides details about the locations, popular dishes, and pricing information to help you savor the authentic flavors of Tennessee.

Nashville:

Edley's Bar-B-Que

- Location: Multiple locations in Nashville, including 12 South, East Nashville, and Sylvan Park.
- Popular Dishes: Try the Tuck Special, a loaded sandwich with smoked chicken, pork, and brisket, or the BBQ Nachos.
- Pricing: Meals generally range from $10 to $15, making it a wallet-friendly option.

Caney Fork River Valley Grille

- Location: 2400 Music Valley Drive, Nashville.
- Popular Dishes: Enjoy the Grille's signature dish, the Big Fork Pork Chop, or the Sampler Platter, which features a variety of smoked meats.
- Pricing: Meals here can range from $20 to $30, offering a heartier dining experience.

Jack's Bar-B-Que

- Location: 416 Broadway, Nashville.
- Popular Dishes: Don't miss the Texas Beef Brisket or the Pork Shoulder Plate.
- Pricing: Jack's is known for its affordable prices, with most dishes falling within the $10 to $15 range.

The Row Kitchen & Pub

- Location: 110 Lyle Avenue, Nashville.
- Popular Dishes: Try their Smoked Brisket Plate or the Smoked BBQ Tacos for a unique twist on traditional barbecue.
- Pricing: Meals generally range from $15 to $25, making it a mid-range option.

The Loveless Cafe

- Location: 8400 TN-100, Nashville.
- Popular Dishes: Savor the Smoked Pork BBQ or indulge in the BBQ Sampler Platter.
- Pricing: Meals typically range from $15 to $25, offering a classic Southern dining experience.

Smokin Thighs - Wedgewood

- Location: 611 Wedgewood Avenue, Nashville.
- Popular Dishes: Experience the mouthwatering Smoked Thighs Plate or the Chicken and Waffle Sandwich.
- Pricing: Most dishes fall within the $10 to $20 range, making it an affordable choice.

Famous Dave's Bar-B-Que

- Location: 5005 Old Hickory Boulevard, Hermitage, Nashville.
- Popular Dishes: Enjoy the All-American BBQ Feast or the St. Louis-Style Spareribs.
- Pricing: Meals are typically priced between $15 and $30, providing a variety of options.

Martin's Bar-B-Que Joint

- Location: Multiple locations in Nashville, including Nolensville Pike, Belmont, and Mount Juliet.
- Popular Dishes: Feast on the Redneck Taco or the Whole Smoked Chicken Platter.
- Pricing: Meals generally range from $15 to $25, offering a delightful barbecue experience.

Butchertown Hall

- Location: 1416 4th Avenue North, Nashville.
- Popular Dishes: Try the Smoked Brisket or the Pulled Pork Sandwich for a unique twist on barbecue classics.
- Pricing: Meals typically range from $15 to $25, making it a mid-

range choice.

Gatlinburg / Pigeon Forge:

Bennett's Pit Bar-B-Que

- Region: Gatlinburg, Tennessee.
- Address: 714 River Road, Gatlinburg.
- Popular Dishes: Try their mouthwatering Pulled Pork Sandwich or the Smoked St. Louis Ribs.
- Pricing: Most meals priced between $15 and $25.

Delauders BBQ

- Region: Pigeon Forge, Tennessee.
- Address: 1791 Middle Creek Road, Sevierville (near Pigeon Forge).
- Popular Dishes: Savor their classic Pulled Pork Plate or opt for the BBQ Sampler to try a bit of everything.
- Pricing: Meals generally falling in the $10 to $20 range.

Hungry Bear BBQ

- Region: Gatlinburg, Tennessee.
- Address: 490 E Parkway, Gatlinburg.
- Popular Dishes: Dive into the Smoked Beef Brisket or the Barbecue Spaghetti for a unique culinary experience.
- Pricing: Most dishes ranging from $10 to $20.

Boss Hogg's BBQ

- Region: Pigeon Forge, Tennessee.

- Address: 1198 Wears Valley Road, Pigeon Forge.
- Popular Dishes: Relish the Pulled Pork Sandwich or the Baby Back Ribs for a classic barbecue feast.
- Pricing: Meals are typically priced between $15 and $25.

Sticky Nicks BBQ

- Region: Gatlinburg, Tennessee.
- Address: 3716 Parkway, Pigeon Forge.
- Popular Dishes: Enjoy their signature Sticky Burger or sample the Hickory-Smoked BBQ Chicken.
- Pricing: Most meals are priced between $10 and $20.

5

Local Restaurants

This chapter is a culinary exploration of the most outstanding local eateries in Tennessee, with a spotlight on Nashville, Gatlinburg, and Pigeon Forge. It delves into the regional flavors, provides addresses, highlights popular dishes, and offers pricing information, ensuring you savor the authentic tastes of Tennessee. This gastronomic guide offers a diverse range of dining experiences from budget-friendly and casual to mid-range and upscale.

Nashville:

Hattie B's Hot Chicken - Midtown

- Address: 112 19th Ave S, Nashville.
- Popular Dishes: Don't miss the legendary Hot Chicken, available in various heat levels. The Southern sides are also a must-try.
- Pricing: Most meals fall in the $10 to $20 range.

Peg Leg Porker

- Address: 903 Gleaves St, Nashville.
- Popular Dishes: Indulge in the Pitmaster Sampler Platter or try the Porker's Pork Sandwich.
- Pricing: Meals typically range from $15 to $25, offering a diverse selection.

Monell's Dining & Catering

- Address: 1235 6th Ave N, Nashville.
- Popular Dishes: Enjoy the Southern-style family dining experience with dishes like Fried Chicken and Biscuits.
- Pricing: Monell's offers an all-inclusive dining experience at around $20 to $40 per person.

1 Kitchen Nashville

- Address: 1000 Main St, Nashville.
- Popular Dishes: Savor the Chef's Tasting Menu, which features seasonal and locally-sourced ingredients.
- Pricing: Offers fine dining experience with pricing typically above $30 per person.

Midtown Cafe

- Address: 102 19th Ave S, Nashville.
- Popular Dishes: Delight in dishes like the Filet Mignon or the Lobster Bisque.
- Pricing: Offers an upscale dining experience with meals generally priced above $30 per person.

Biscuit Love

- Address: Multiple locations, including the Gulch and Hillsboro Village.
- Popular Dishes: Sample the Bonuts, a delightful biscuit and donut hybrid, or the East Nasty biscuit sandwich.
- Pricing: Most dishes are priced between $10 and $15.

Pancake Pantry

- Address: 1796 21st Ave S, Nashville.
- Popular Dishes: Enjoy a wide variety of pancakes, including the Caribbean Pancakes or Sweet Potato Pancakes.
- Pricing: Meals are typically budget-friendly, ranging from $10 to $20.

Arnold's Country Kitchen

- Address: 605 8th Ave S, Nashville.
- Popular Dishes: Relish a daily-changing menu of Southern classics, including Meatloaf and Fried Chicken.
- Pricing: Most meals fall in the $10 to $15 range.

Gatlinburg / Pigeon Forge:

Pancake Pantry

- Region: Gatlinburg, Tennessee.
- Address: 628 Parkway, Gatlinburg.
- Popular Dishes: Savor a variety of pancakes, from Wild Berry to Apricot-Lemon Delight.
- Pricing: Most meals are priced between $10 and $20.

Bennett's Pit Bar-B-Que

- Region: Gatlinburg, Tennessee.
- Address: 714 River Road, Gatlinburg.
- Popular Dishes: Try the Pulled Pork Sandwich or the Smoked St. Louis Ribs.
- Pricing: Most meals are priced between $15 and $25.

Crockett's 1875 Breakfast Camp

- Region: Gatlinburg, Tennessee.
- Address: 1103 Parkway, Gatlinburg.
- Popular Dishes: Enjoy the Camp Breakfast Skillet or the Wild Griddle Cakes.
- Pricing: Most dishes ranging from $10 to $20.

Chesapeake's - Gatlinburg

- Region: Gatlinburg, Tennessee.
- Address: 437 E Parkway, Gatlinburg.
- Popular Dishes: Savor the Seafood Platter or the Maryland Crab Cakes.
- Pricing: Most meals are typically priced between $15 and $30.

Smoky Mountain Trout House

- Region: Gatlinburg, Tennessee.
- Address: 410 Parkway, Gatlinburg.
- Popular Dishes: Enjoy the Grilled Mountain Trout or the Seafood Platter.
- Pricing: Most meals are priced between $20 to $30 per person.

LOCAL RESTAURANTS

Local Goat

- Region: Pigeon Forge, Tennessee.
- Address: 2167 Parkway, Pigeon Forge.
- Popular Dishes: Relish the Farm-to-Table offerings, such as the Goat Cheese Stuffed Chicken or the Bison Meatloaf.
- Pricing: Most meals are priced between $15 and $25.

Old Mill Restaurant

- Region: Pigeon Forge, Tennessee.
- Address: 164 Old Mill Ave, Pigeon Forge.
- Popular Dishes: Delight in the Southern Fried Chicken or the Pot Roast.
- Pricing: Most meals are priced around $15 to $25 per person.

Sawyer's Farmhouse Breakfast

- Region: Pigeon Forge, Tennessee.
- Address: 2831 Parkway, Pigeon Forge.
- Popular Dishes: Enjoy hearty breakfast options, such as the Farmhouse Omelette or the Cinnamon Roll Pancakes.
- Pricing: Most dishes are priced between $10 and $20.

Brick and Spoon

- Region: Pigeon Forge, Tennessee.
- Address: 2726 Parkway, Pigeon Forge.
- Popular Dishes: Explore a diverse breakfast menu with dishes like the Cajun Breakfast Skillet or the Bourbon Street Benedict.
- Pricing: Most meals ranging from $15 to $30.

Timberwood Grill

- Region: Pigeon Forge, Tennessee.
- Address: 131 The Island Dr, Pigeon Forge.
- Popular Dishes: Savor the Timberwood Trout or the Smoky Mountain Brisket.
- Pricing: Most meals are priced between $15 and $30.

6

Tours

Listed below are the best tours in Tennessee, whether you're exploring the vibrant streets of Nashville or immersing yourself in the natural beauty of the Great Smoky Mountains in Gatlinburg and Pigeon Forge. Your guide to the best tours offering descriptions of the tours, pricing information, details about parking, and additional helpful advice to consider before booking.

Nashville:

TENNESSEE: TRAVEL GUIDE

Hop-on Hop-off Trolley Tour

- Description: Explore Nashville's iconic landmarks at your own pace with the flexibility of hopping on and off the trolley. Enjoy informative narration about the city's history and culture.
- Pricing: Prices typically range from $50 - $75 per adult ticket and $25 per child.
- Duration: At your own pace approx 6 hours
- Parking Info: Many trolley tours depart from convenient locations with parking nearby. It's advisable to arrive early to secure a parking spot.

Double-Decker City Tour

- Description: Experience Nashville from an open-top double-decker bus, offering great views of the city's attractions. Learn

about the city's history and music scene during this guided tour.
- Pricing: Tickets generally from $40 for adults and $30 for children.
- Duration: Approx 1 hour
- Parking Info: Parking facilities are often available near the tour departure points. Be sure to arrive early for parking convenience.

Night Tour of Music City

- Description: Discover Nashville's vibrant nightlife on a guided night tour. Witness the city's illuminated landmarks and enjoy live music along the way.
- Pricing: Tickets usually range from $50 to $70 per adult and $45 per child.
- Duration: Approx 1.5 hours
- Parking Info: Check with the tour provider for parking recommendations or available parking facilities near the departure point.

Homes of the Stars Narrated Bus Tour

- Description: Get a glimpse of the residences of Nashville's famous personalities. A narrated tour offers insights into the city's celebrity culture.
- Pricing: Prices generally from $65 per adult and $33 per child.
- Duration: Approx 2 hours
- Parking Info: Arrangements for parking may vary, so consider inquiring with the tour operator about parking options.

Grand Ole Opry Backstage Tour

- Description: Embark on a guided tour behind the scenes of the legendary Grand Ole Opry. Explore the dressing rooms, stage, and

experience the magic of country music history.
- Pricing: Tickets usually range from $40 to $50 per adult and $30 to $40 per child.
- Duration: Approx 1 hour
- Parking Info: Parking at the Grand Ole Opry may require a fee, so be prepared for this cost.

RCA Studio B & Country Music Hall of Fame Combo

- Description: This combo tour takes you to RCA Studio B, where Elvis Presley recorded, and the Country Music Hall of Fame. Experience the heart of country music history.
- Pricing: Prices from $49.95 per adult and $39.95 per child.
- Duration: Approx 2-5 hours
- Parking Info: Both attractions have parking facilities, and costs may apply. Consider budgeting for parking fees.

The Ville All-Inclusive Pub Crawl

- Description: Enjoy a lively night out with this all-inclusive pub crawl, visiting some of Nashville's most popular bars and enjoying music and local beverages.
- Pricing: Tickets generally from $69 per adult.
- Duration: Approx 2 hours
- Parking Info: Since this tour involves alcohol consumption, it's recommended to arrange transportation to and from the starting point to ensure a safe evening.

Gulch & Union Station: Walking & Tasting Food Tour

- Description: Stroll through Nashville's Gulch and Union Station

neighborhoods while sampling a variety of local cuisines. Learn about the city's culinary scene.
- Pricing: Prices usually from $89 per adult.
- Duration: Approx 3 hours
- Parking Info: Some tours offer complimentary parking or provide information about nearby parking facilities.

From Nashville: Lynchburg Jack Daniel's Distillery Tour

- Description: Venture to the Jack Daniel's Distillery in Lynchburg for a guided tour, including a tasting experience. Learn about the whiskey-making process.
- Pricing: Prices generally from $159 per adult.
- Duration: Approx 7 hours
- Parking Info: The distillery typically offers parking for visitors.

Gatlinburg / Pigeon Forge:

The "Classic" National Park Tour

- Description: Explore the Great Smoky Mountains National Park with a guided tour, offering insights into the park's natural beauty and history.
- Pricing: Tickets usually from $150 per adult.
- Duration: Approx 3 hours
- Parking Info: Parking is often available at or near the tour's departure location.

Sights of Smoky Mountains with Lunch Included

- Description: Experience the stunning sights of the Smoky Moun-

tains with a guided tour that includes lunch. Learn about the park's ecosystem and history.
- Pricing: Prices generally range from $130 per adult and $85 per child.
- Duration: Approx 6 hours
- Parking Info: Many tours depart from locations with accessible parking.

Great Smoky Mountains National Park Self Driving Tour

- Description: Enjoy a self-guided driving tour of the national park, offering flexibility and a chance to explore at your own pace.
- Pricing: Entrance to the park is usually $25 per vehicle.
- Duration: Approx 2–3 hours
- Parking Info: Parking is available at various points within the park.

High Points Driving Tour

- Description: Discover the high points and overlooks of the Great Smoky Mountains on this driving tour, offering panoramic views of the region.
- Pricing: Entrance to the park is typically $150 per adult.
- Duration: Approx 3 hours
- Parking Info: Parking is available at designated overlooks within the park.

Thundering Streams and Falls of the Smokies Guided Hiking Tour

- Description: Embark on a guided hiking tour to explore the cascading waterfalls and streams of the Smoky Mountains. Learn about the park's ecology.

- Pricing: Tickets usually range from $76 per adult and $68 per child.
- Duration: Approx 3 hours
- Parking Info: Parking is often available at trailheads within the national park.

Great Smoky Mountains National Park and Cades Cove Self-Driving Bundle Tours

- Description: This bundle includes self-driving tours of the Great Smoky Mountains and Cades Cove, providing a comprehensive park experience.
- Pricing: Entrance to the park is generally $25 per vehicle.
- Duration: Approx 3–5 hours
- Parking Info: Parking is available at various points within the park.

Old Growth Forest Cascade

- Description: Explore old-growth forests and cascading waterfalls in the Smoky Mountains on this guided nature tour.
- Pricing: Tickets typically from $175 per person.
- Duration: Approx 8 hours
- Parking Info: Parking is available at trailheads within the national park.

7

Local Attractions

This comprehensive guide to the best local attractions in Tennessee, whether you're in the heart of Nashville or exploring the enchanting landscapes of Gatlinburg and Pigeon Forge is your guide to the most captivating attractions in major cities in Tennessee, providing descriptions of the attractions, pricing information, details about parking.

Nashville:

Grand Ole Opry Show Ticket

- Description: Experience the world-renowned Grand Ole Opry, showcasing the best of country music. Enjoy live performances by top artists.
- Pricing: Ticket prices typically range from $40 to $80 per person.
- Parking Info: The Grand Ole Opry has on-site parking available. Be sure to check for parking fees.

Country Music Hall of Fame and Museum

- Description: Explore the rich history of country music with exhibits, artifacts, and interactive displays. Immerse yourself in the music that made Nashville famous.
- Pricing: Admission prices generally range from $25 to $40 per adult.

- Parking Info: Parking is available in nearby lots, and costs may apply.

Zoo: Skip-the-Line Admission Ticket

- Description: Visit the Nashville Zoo and skip the lines for a seamless experience. Encounter a variety of animals and engage in wildlife conservation.
- Pricing: Skip-the-line admission typically ranges from $20 to $30 per person.
- Parking Info: The zoo provides parking facilities, often with a nominal fee.

Johnny Cash Museum

- Description: Step into the life and legacy of the legendary Johnny Cash. The museum showcases memorabilia, artifacts, and insights into his iconic career.
- Pricing: Admission prices usually range from $25 to $35 per adult and $20 to $30 per child.
- Parking Info: Check for nearby parking options or garages close to the museum.

Patsy Cline Museum

- Description: Delve into the world of Patsy Cline, one of country music's greatest stars. Explore her life and contributions to the genre.
- Pricing: Admission to the museum typically costs from $21.95 per adult and $17.95 per child.
- Parking Info: Look for parking facilities nearby, as street parking

can be limited.

Music City Center

- Description: Visit the Music City Center, a premier convention center in Nashville. Explore events, conventions, and exhibitions.
- Pricing: Admission to events varies; check specific event listings for pricing.
- Parking Info: The Music City Center offers on-site parking, which may have varying rates depending on the event.

Union Station

- Description: Discover the historic Union Station Hotel, known for its stunning architecture and luxury accommodations. Explore the lobby's beauty.
- Pricing: Free to enter and explore; costs apply if you plan to stay in the hotel.
- Parking Info: The hotel offers parking, but be sure to inquire about pricing and availability.

Ryman Auditorium

- Description: Visit the "Mother Church of Country Music," a beloved music venue known for its incredible acoustics and legendary performances.
- Pricing: Tours typically range from $25 to $35 per adult, check specific tour listings for pricing.
- Parking Info: Self-Parking for all Ryman events is available directly across the street and parking can be purchased upon entering the garage.

Musicians Hall of Fame

- Description: Explore the achievements and contributions of musicians across genres. The museum celebrates music legends and their instruments.
- Pricing: Admission from $28 per adult and $15 per youth.
- Parking Info: Check for nearby parking facilities or garages.

Bicentennial Capitol State Park

- Description: Immerse yourself in Tennessee's history at this beautiful park. Enjoy scenic views, monuments, and learn about the state's heritage.
- Pricing: Free to enter and explore.
- Parking Info: Parking is available at the park, and it is typically free of charge.

Tennessee State Library & Archives

- Description: Discover the extensive collection of historical documents, manuscripts, and genealogical resources. Delve into Tennessee's past.
- Pricing: Access to the library and archives is free of charge.
- Parking Info: The facility offers on-site parking for visitors.

Tennessee State Museum

- Description: Dive into Tennessee's history through exhibits and artifacts, showcasing the state's cultural and political evolution.
- Pricing: Admission to the museum is generally free, making it an excellent value.

- Parking Info: There are parking options near the museum; some may require fees. Free parking is available in the lot shared by the Museum and the Farmers' Market.

Andrew Jackson's Hermitage

- Description: Visit the historic home of President Andrew Jackson. Explore the mansion, gardens, and the legacy of the seventh president.
- Pricing: Tickets typically range from $20 per adult and $13 per youth..
- Parking Info: The Hermitage provides free parking for visitors.

Marathon Motor Works

- Description: Discover the history of the Marathon Motor Works and its transformation into a creative and artistic hub.
- Pricing: Admission is typically free; costs may apply for specific events.
- Parking Info: There are parking facilities nearby.

The Parthenon

- Description: Explore a full-scale replica of the Parthenon in Athens. Admire art, sculptures, and the beauty of Centennial Park.
- Pricing: Admission typically ranges from $8 to $10 per adult and $8 for youth.
- Parking Info: Centennial Park offers parking facilities, often with a nominal fee.

Vanderbilt University

- Description: Discover the beautiful Vanderbilt University campus, known for its stunning architecture and vibrant academic community.
- Pricing: Free to explore the campus grounds.
- Parking Info: There are parking options near the university.

Belmont Mansion

- Description: Visit the Belmont Mansion, a historic site that offers guided tours of the antebellum estate and its rich history.
- Pricing: Tickets typically range from $13 to $45 per adult, $6 per child and $8 per youth
- Parking Info: The mansion provides free parking for visitors.

Gatlinburg / Pigeon Forge:

Dollywood

- Description: Experience Dollywood, an award-winning theme park featuring thrilling rides, live entertainment, and the charm of the Smoky Mountains.
- Pricing: Admission prices typically range from $79 to $89 per person and $79 per child.
- Parking Info: Dollywood offers on-site parking, with costs varying by vehicle type.

Dollywood's Splash Country (Seasonal)

- Description: Cool off at Dollywood's Splash Country, a water park offering water rides and attractions for all ages.
- Pricing: Admission typically ranges from $45 to $55 per person.
- Parking Info: Parking facilities are available at Splash Country, with fees based on vehicle type.

Hatfield and McCoy Dinner Show in Pigeon Forge

- Description: Enjoy a lively dinner show that tells the story of the Hatfield and McCoy feud with humor, music, and a delicious meal.
- Pricing: Show prices usually range from $59.99 to $80 per adult and $34.99 per child.
- Parking Info: The venue typically provides parking options.

Dolly Parton's Stampede Dinner Show

- Description: Experience a thrilling dinner show featuring equestrian stunts, music, and a delicious four-course meal.
- Pricing: Show prices generally range from $59.99 to $83.99 per

adult and $34.99 to $44.99 per child.
- Parking Info: The venue typically offers parking options.

Steven Best's Unbelievable Magic Shows Pigeon Forge, TN

- Description: Be amazed by incredible magic tricks and illusions performed by magician Steven Best in Pigeon Forge.
- Pricing: Ticket prices usually range from $39 per adult and $10 per child.
- Parking Info: Parking facilities are often available at or near the show venue.

Wild Stallion Alpine Mountain Coaster Pigeon Forge Coaster

- Description: Experience the thrill of the Wild Stallion Alpine Mountain Coaster with exciting twists, turns, and scenic mountain views.
- Pricing: Ride prices typically range from $18.99 per adult and $9.99 per person. (Scenic chair lift not included.)
- Parking Info: The coaster site typically offers parking.

Country Tonite Theater In Pigeon Forge, TN

- Description: Enjoy a high-energy variety show with music, comedy, and dancing at the Country Tonite Theater in Pigeon Forge.
- Pricing: Show prices usually range from $30 to $50 per person.
- Parking Info: The theater typically provides parking facilities.

Paula Deen's Lumberjack Feud Dinner Show

- Description: Witness thrilling lumberjack competitions and enjoy

a delicious meal at Paula Deen's Lumberjack Feud Dinner Show.
- Pricing: Show prices typically range from $56 per adult and $22 per child.
- Parking Info: The venue typically offers parking options.

Pirates Voyage Dinner & Show in Pigeon Forge, TN

- Description: Set sail on an adventure with Pirates Voyage Dinner & Show, featuring swashbuckling pirates, mermaids, and a delectable meal.
- Pricing: Show prices generally range from $59.99 per adult and from $34.99 per child.
- Parking Info: The venue typically provides parking options.

The Redneck Comedy Bus Tour Pigeon Forge

- Description: Laugh out loud on the Redneck Comedy Bus Tour in Pigeon Forge, an entertaining journey through the Smoky Mountains.
- Pricing: Ticket prices usually range from $35 per adult and $30 per child.
- Parking Info: Parking facilities are available at the tour departure point.

Elvis & The Superstars Pigeon Forge

- Description: Enjoy a tribute show featuring performances by Elvis Presley and other music legends in Pigeon Forge.
- Pricing: Show prices typically range from $39 per adult and $14 per child.
- Parking Info: Parking is usually available at or near the show venue.

Smoky Mountains Jeep Tours in Pigeon Forge

- Description: Explore the beauty of the Smoky Mountains on a guided Jeep tour, providing access to scenic locations.
- Pricing: Tour prices typically range from $40 to $50 per person.
- Parking Info: Check with the tour provider for parking information.

Anakeesta Mountain Sightseeing Chondola in Pigeon Forge

- Description: Ride the Chondola to Anakeesta Mountain for breathtaking views of the Smoky Mountains, treetop adventures, and dining options.
- Pricing: Chondola ride and park admission usually range from $65 per adult.
- Parking Info: The park provides parking facilities.

Rocky Top Mountain Coaster Pigeon Forge

- Description: Experience the thrill of the Rocky Top Mountain Coaster with a combination of dips, twists, and turns, day or night.
- Pricing: Ride prices typically range from $18 per adult and $14 per child.
- Parking Info: The coaster site usually offers parking.

RainForest Adventures Discovery Zoo Pigeon Forge

- Description: Visit RainForest Adventures Discovery Zoo in Pigeon Forge to encounter a variety of exotic animals and learn about their habitats.
- Pricing: Admission typically ranges from $16.99 per adult and

$9.99 per child.
- Parking Info: Parking facilities are often available at the zoo.

Hollywood Wax Museum Pigeon Forge, TN

- Description: Explore the Hollywood Wax Museum in Pigeon Forge, featuring lifelike wax figures of celebrities from film and television.
- Pricing: Admission prices generally range from $39.99 per adult and $19.99 per child.
- Parking Info: The museum offers parking facilities.

Smoky Mountain Helicopter Tours - Helicopter Rides in Pigeon Forge, TN

- Description: Soar above the Smoky Mountains on a thrilling helicopter tour, providing breathtaking aerial views of the natural beauty.
- Pricing: Tour prices usually range from $126.14 per person.
- Parking Info: The tour provider typically offers parking facilities.

Gatlinburg Space Needle

- Description: Ascend the Gatlinburg Space Needle for panoramic views of the city and the surrounding Smoky Mountains.
- Pricing: Admission typically ranges from $15.95 per adult and $9.95 per child.
- Parking Info: The attraction offers parking facilities.

SkyLand Ranch & Horizon SkyRide Skylift

- Description: Explore the beauty of the Smoky Mountains on the

SkyRide Skylift, offering stunning vistas and adventure at SkyLand Ranch.
- Pricing: Ride and park admission usually range from $21.99 per adult and $12.99 per child.
- Parking Info: The attraction provides parking facilities.

Gatlinburg SkyBridge

- Description: Cross the Gatlinburg SkyBridge, one of the world's longest pedestrian suspension bridges, for breathtaking mountain views.
- Pricing: Admission typically ranges from $31.95 per adult and $22.95 per junior.
- Parking Info: There are parking facilities available at the attraction.

Anakeesta's Rail Runner Mountain Coaster

- Description: Experience the thrill of the Rail Runner Mountain Coaster at Anakeesta, offering a high-speed, gravity-propelled adventure.
- Pricing: Ride and park admission typically range from $34.99 per adult and $22.99 per child.
- Parking Info: The park provides parking facilities.

8

Local Bars

Local bars in Nashville, Gatlinburg and Pigeon Forge offer a range of experiences from live music to casual lounges, ensuring you find the perfect spot for a memorable evening. Take in the historic sites and bars of Nashville located on Broadway. This is the place to go for live music, dancing and drinking that are within walking distance from most hotels. There's no cover charge at honky tonk bars but the musicians survive on tips and most take requests. Most honky tonks are open to all ages until 6pm. Some switch to 21+ at 8pm, others at 10pm.

Nashville:

The Bluebird Café
　Experience the intimate setting of The Bluebird Café, a renowned live music venue that has hosted many legendary artists. Admission prices vary based on performances, so check their schedule. Limited free parking is available; consider arriving early or walking from your hotel.

Tootsie's Orchid Lounge

Visit the historic Tootsie's Orchid Lounge, known as the "purple palace of good times." Enjoy live country music and a vibrant atmosphere. Prices for food and drinks depend on your selections. Check for nearby parking options; public parking garages are available or walking from your hotel.

Robert's Western World

Dive into the heart of honky-tonk at Robert's Western World. Enjoy live music, dancing, and classic country vibes. Prices for food, drinks, and live music may vary. There are parking lots and garages nearby or consider walking from your hotel.

The Stage

Immerse yourself in the energy of The Stage, offering live music, a lively crowd, and a great atmosphere for dancing. Prices for food, drinks, and cover charges vary based on events. Public parking garages are available close by.

Big Bang Dueling Piano Bar

Enjoy an entertaining night at the Big Bang Dueling Piano Bar, where pianists perform requests and create a lively show. Cover charges may apply; drinks and food prices vary. Public parking garages are nearby or consider walking from your hotel.

Legends Corner

Visit Legends Corner, a classic honky-tonk bar with live country music and a relaxed atmosphere. Food, drinks, and cover charges may vary. Public parking options are available in the area or consider walking from your hotel.

Wildhorse Saloon

Wildhorse Saloon offers live music, dancing, and Southern cuisine. It's a lively destination for a fun night out. No over charges may apply; food and drinks prices vary. Public parking garages are nearby or consider walking.

Kid Rock's Big Ass Honky Tonk Rock N' Roll Steakhouse

Enjoy the unique blend of music and food at Kid Rock's Honky Tonk. It's a lively spot with a rock 'n' roll atmosphere. Prices for food, drinks, and live music may vary. Public parking garages are nearby or consider walking.

Jason Aldean's Kitchen + Rooftop Bar: My Kinda Party

Jason Aldean's Kitchen + Rooftop Bar offers a rooftop experience with great food, drinks, and live music. Food, drinks, and live music prices may vary. Public parking garages are available nearby or consider walking.

The Second Fiddle

Visit The Second Fiddle, a classic honky-tonk bar with live music, a friendly atmosphere, and dancing. Food, drinks, and cover charges may vary. Public parking options are nearby.

Gatlinburg / Pigeon Forge:

Ole Red Gatlinburg

Experience Ole Red Gatlinburg, a lively venue with live music, great food, and a welcoming Southern vibe. Prices for food, drinks, and cover charges vary. Check for nearby parking facilities.

Tennessee Cider Company

Enjoy the locally crafted ciders at Tennessee Cider Company. It's a great spot to savor unique flavors. Cider prices vary, and they offer tastings. Look for nearby parking options.

Ole Smoky Moonshine Distillery

Explore the Ole Smoky Moonshine Distillery, where you can taste a variety of moonshines and enjoy the lively atmosphere. Moonshine tasting prices may vary. The distillery often provides parking options or street parking.

Loft Lounge

The Loft Lounge offers a relaxed setting to unwind and enjoy drinks with friends. Prices for drinks and snacks may vary. Check for parking facilities nearby.

Landshark Bar & Grill

Visit Landshark Bar & Grill for a fun and casual dining experience with beach-themed vibes. Prices for food and drinks vary. Parking is available at the venue.

Gatlinburg SkyCenter

Enjoy the Gatlinburg SkyCenter for breathtaking mountain views and a unique observation experience. Admission prices vary; check their website for details. Parking is available on-site.

Cliff Top

Cliff Top offers a scenic location to enjoy drinks and the beauty of the Smoky Mountains. Prices for drinks may vary. Check for parking facilities nearby.

Iron Boar Saloon

Visit Iron Boar Saloon for a welcoming atmosphere, live music, and Southern hospitality. Prices for food, drinks, and cover charges may vary. Public parking options are nearby.

Smoky Mountain Brewery
Smoky Mountain Brewery offers a taste of locally crafted beers and a relaxed setting for socializing. Prices for beers and food may vary. Parking facilities are typically available.

Shamrock Pub
The Shamrock Pub is a friendly and traditional Irish pub, offering a warm atmosphere and a selection of drinks. Prices for drinks and snacks may vary. Look for parking options nearby.

Margaritaville Resort
Margaritaville Resort is known for its island-inspired vibes, drinks, and entertainment, making it a perfect escape. Prices for drinks and food may vary. The resort often provides parking facilities.

The Fox & Parrot Tavern
The Fox & Parrot Tavern offers a taste of England with a wide selection of beers and a cozy, British pub atmosphere. Prices for beers and food may vary. Check for parking facilities nearby.

Jason Aldean's Kitchen + Rooftop Bar
Jason Aldean's Kitchen + Rooftop Bar in Pigeon Forge offers a rooftop experience with great food, drinks, and live music. Food, drinks, and live music prices may vary. Public parking garages are available nearby or street parking.

Sugarlands Distilling Co

Explore the Sugarlands Distilling Co to taste a variety of locally crafted spirits and enjoy the distillery experience. Spirits tasting prices may vary. The distillery often provides parking options.

The Greenbrier Restaurant

The Greenbrier Restaurant offers a fine dining experience with a varied menu and a cozy ambiance. Prices for food and drinks may vary. Check for parking facilities nearby.

Old Forge Distillery

Discover the Old Forge Distillery, offering tastings of locally crafted spirits and a glimpse into the distillation process. Spirits tasting prices may vary. The distillery often provides parking options.

9

Nightlife and Live Music

Whether you're in Nashville or the Gatlinburg / Pigeon Forge area, you'll find a variety of options to enjoy the rhythm of the South. The vibrant nightlife of Tennessee, focuses on local bars and venues with live music and dancing. Your gateway to the lively nightlife; get ready to enjoy the rhythm and energy of the live music scene in these major cities and towns.

Nashville:

The Bluebird Café

The Bluebird Café offers an intimate setting for live music performances and a chance to enjoy emerging artists. Arrive early to secure a seat; reservations are recommended for some events.

Tootsie's Orchid Lounge

Tootsie's Orchid Lounge, a historic honky-tonk bar, features live country music and a lively dance floor. The venue may get crowded, so arrive early for a good spot.

Robert's Western World

Robert's Western World is a classic honky-tonk bar with live music, dancing, and a memorable Western atmosphere. Enjoy the unique Western vibe and join the dance floor.

The Stage

NIGHTLIFE AND LIVE MUSIC

The Stage is known for live music, a bustling dance floor, and a fantastic atmosphere for a night of fun. Check their event calendar for featured artists.

Big Bang Dueling Piano Bar

Big Bang Dueling Piano Bar offers an entertaining show with talented pianists taking song requests. Be prepared for interactive and lively performances.

Legends Corner

Legends Corner is a classic honky-tonk bar with live country music and a friendly atmosphere. Get your dancing shoes ready.

Wildhorse Saloon

Wildhorse Saloon offers live music, line dancing, and Southern cuisine for an unforgettable night. Join the dance lessons to learn some moves.

Kid Rock's Big Ass Honky Tonk Rock N' Roll Steakhouse

Kid Rock's Honky Tonk offers a unique blend of rock 'n' roll music, delicious food, and a lively rooftop bar. Don't miss the rooftop bar for great views.

Jason Aldean's Kitchen + Rooftop Bar: My Kinda Party

Jason Aldean's Kitchen + Rooftop Bar combines great food, live music, and a rooftop experience. Enjoy a meal and then head to the rooftop for music.

The Second Fiddle

The Second Fiddle is a classic honky-tonk bar with live music and a friendly atmosphere. Check out their daily live music schedule.

Grand Ole Opry Show

The Grand Ole Opry Show offers a legendary live country music experience, featuring various artists. Book tickets in advance for a seat at this iconic venue.

Gatlinburg / Pigeon Forge:

Gatlinburg downtown

Gatlinburg's downtown area offers various bars and venues with live music and nightlife. Explore the downtown scene for different options.

Gatlinburg Barrelhouse

The Gatlinburg Barrelhouse offers live music in a comfortable setting, perfect for a night out. Enjoy the music while savoring drinks and food.

Hogg's Upstairs Taverne

Hogg's Upstairs Taverne provides a cozy atmosphere with live music and a selection of beverages. It's a great place to unwind after a day of exploring.

Ghostwalk of Gatlinburg

The Ghostwalk of Gatlinburg is an intriguing and unique nighttime tour experience. Book your tour in advance for a captivating evening.

Smoky Mountain Brewery

Smoky Mountain Brewery is known for craft beers and live music, creating a relaxed and social atmosphere. Enjoy a variety of craft beers.

Tennessee Cider Company

Tennessee Cider Company offers locally crafted ciders and a pleasant place to enjoy them. Taste unique cider flavors.

Ole Smoky Moonshine Distillery

Explore the Ole Smoky Moonshine Distillery for moonshine tastings and a lively environment. Try different moonshine flavors.

Gatlinburg Space Needle

Ascend the Gatlinburg Space Needle for impressive views and a unique nighttime observation experience. The nighttime views are especially breathtaking.

Smith and Son Corner Kitchen

Smith and Son Corner Kitchen offers a cozy setting for drinks, snacks, and a relaxed evening. Enjoy their menu offerings with friends.

Funky Budha

Funky Budha is a welcoming place for a night out, with a selection of beverages and live music. Check their event schedule for live music nights.

Anakeesta's at night

Anakeesta offers nighttime experiences with picturesque views, treehouse adventures, and dining options. The nighttime atmosphere is enchanting.

10

Family Friendly Activities

These kid-friendly activities in Nashville and Gatlinburg/Pigeon Forge are sure to keep your little ones entertained, creating lasting family memories and ensuring that your vacation is filled with fun and memorable experiences for all ages.

Nashville:

Hop-on Hop-off Trolley Tour
Explore Nashville's key landmarks on a convenient trolley tour, allowing you to hop on and off at various stops.

Zoo: Skip-the-Line Admission Ticket
Visit the Nashville Zoo for a day of wildlife exploration, and skip the lines with your admission ticket.

Country Music Hall of Fame and Museum
Immerse yourself in the history of country music at the Country Music Hall of Fame and Museum.

Bicentennial Capitol State Park
Bicentennial Capitol State Park offers a beautiful space with historical and educational elements for family enjoyment.

The Parthenon
Explore a full-scale replica of the Parthenon in Nashville, an educational and architectural marvel.

Sightseeing Cart Tour
Enjoy a sightseeing cart tour that offers a guided exploration of Nashville's landmarks and history.

1-Hour Escape Room Adventure in Berry Hill
Engage in an exciting and challenging escape room adventure in Berry Hill, providing family-friendly entertainment.

Gatlinburg / Pigeon Forge:

Dollywood

Dollywood offers thrilling rides, entertainment, and family fun in a picturesque mountain setting.

FAMILY FRIENDLY ACTIVITIES

Dollywood's Splash Country (Seasonal)
Dollywood's Splash Country is a water park with slides and attractions, perfect for a refreshing family day.

Hatfield and McCoy Dinner Show in Pigeon Forge
The Hatfield and McCoy Dinner Show offers comedic performances and a delicious dinner for family entertainment.

Dolly Parton's Stampede Dinner Show
Experience the Dolly Parton's Stampede Dinner Show, featuring horse performances and a hearty meal.

Steven Best's Unbelievable Magic Shows Pigeon Forge, TN
Enjoy the magic and illusions of Steven Best's Unbelievable Magic Show for a captivating family experience.

Wild Stallion Alpine Mountain Coaster Pigeon Forge Coaster
Experience the Wild Stallion Alpine Mountain Coaster for an exhilarating ride through the mountains.

Country Tonite Theater In Pigeon Forge, TN
The Country Tonite Theater offers family-friendly entertainment, including music, comedy, and more.

Paula Deen's Lumberjack Feud Dinner Show
Paula Deen's Lumberjack Feud Dinner Show offers thrilling lumberjack competitions and a delicious dinner.

Pirates Voyage Dinner & Show in Pigeon Forge, TN
Experience the Pirates Voyage Dinner & Show for a swashbuckling adventure and a tasty meal.

The Redneck Comedy Bus Tour Pigeon Forge
Embark on the Redneck Comedy Bus Tour for laughter and sightseeing in Pigeon Forge.

Elvis & The Superstars Pigeon Forge
Enjoy Elvis & The Superstars, a tribute show featuring talented artists and iconic music.

Smoky Mountains Jeep Tours in Pigeon Forge
Explore the Smoky Mountains with guided Jeep tours, providing scenic adventures for the family.

Anakeesta Mountain Sightseeing Chondola in Pigeon Forge
The Anakeesta Mountain Sightseeing Chondola offers breathtaking mountain views and activities for all ages.

Rocky Top Mountain Coaster Pigeon Forge
Ride the Rocky Top Mountain Coaster for an exciting family adventure in the heart of the Smoky Mountains.

RainForest Adventures Discovery Zoo Pigeon Forge
Visit RainForest Adventures Discovery Zoo for a unique wildlife experience with exotic animals.

Hollywood Wax Museum Pigeon Forge, TN
Explore the Hollywood Wax Museum for a fun and interactive experience with lifelike celebrity wax figures.

Smoky Mountain Helicopter Tours - Helicopter Rides in Pigeon Forge, TN
Take a thrilling helicopter ride with Smoky Mountain Helicopter

FAMILY FRIENDLY ACTIVITIES

Tours to see the stunning landscapes from above.

Gatlinburg Space Needle
Visit the Gatlinburg Space Needle for breathtaking panoramic views of the Smoky Mountains and the city.

Gatlinburg downtown
Gatlinburg's downtown area offers various family-friendly activities, including shops, restaurants, and attractions.

SkyLand Ranch & Horizon SkyRide Skylift
SkyLand Ranch & Horizon SkyRide Skylift offers a chairlift ride and stunning views of Gatlinburg and the mountains.

Gatlinburg SkyBridge
Walk across the Gatlinburg SkyBridge, a scenic and thrilling experience offering fantastic views.

Anakeesta's Rail Runner Mountain Coaster
Enjoy the Anakeesta's Rail Runner Mountain Coaster, a thrilling ride through the forested mountainside.

Smokey Mountain Excursions
Smokey Mountain Excursions offer guided adventures and outdoor experiences for the whole family.

11

Conclusion

As we bring your Middle Tennessee journey to a close and as you reflect on the pages you've turned, remember the remarkable places and experiences you've encountered in this vibrant region. The landscapes, the flavors, and the people have all contributed to creating moments you'll treasure for a lifetime.

As you prepare to bid farewell to Middle Tennessee, consider these parting words of wisdom: Keep an open heart and mind as you travel, embracing the local culture and savoring the uniqueness of each place you visit. These are the keys to truly immersing yourself in your journey and making it a one-of-a-kind experience.

I want to express my sincere gratitude for choosing this guidebook as your companion on this adventure. Your trust and readership have been deeply appreciated. As you turn the final page, I invite you to share your feedback and your own experiences with me. Your insights are invaluable, helping future travelers embark on their journeys with confidence.

CONCLUSION

As this journey concludes, remember that it's not the end but merely a pause in your explorations. Countless more adventures await you, each one a new chapter in the story of your life. So keep turning those pages, keep exploring, and keep creating unforgettable memories. Your next adventure is just around the corner.

Printed in Great Britain
by Amazon